Rub-a-Dub

A Phonics Reader

By Sasha Quinton

The Book Shop, Ltd.
New York, New York

© 2009 The Book Shop, Ltd
Photographs © Juniperimages Corporation

Rub-a-**dub-dub.** It's time for the **tub.**

This **muddy pup** needs a good **scrub.**

Fur full of **dust,** he's covered with **mud.**
Fill **up** the **tub. Put** in some **suds.**

Grab a big **brush. Scrub**-a-**dub-dub.**
Make sure you give this **pup** a good **rub.**

Plunk! What's this? Who **jumped** in the **tub?**

Plunk!

Another **grubby pup** needs a good **rub.**

Two **sudsy puppies** are better than **one.**
Rub-a-pup-pup is double the **fun.**

Two **sudsy pups** rinse off with a **jug.**

They **jump** from the **tub.** They shake on the **rug.**

One **bumps** the **tub.** It makes a loud **thud.**
It **dumps** on the **rug.** It causes a **flood.**

Thud!

What a big mess! There are **suds** on the **rug.**
Clean **up** the **bubbles. Scrub**-a-**dub**-**rug.**

One chilly **pup** wraps **up** in the **rug.**

One **jumps** into bed, as **snug** as a **bug.**

Two little **pups** want another **fun scrub.**
So **rub-a-dub-dub! Put** them back in the **tub!**